Mixing

Patricia Whitehouse

www.raintreepublishers.co.uk

Visit our website to find out more information about **Raintree** books.

To order:

☎ Phone 44 (0) 1865 888112

📄 Send a fax to 44 (0) 1865 314091

💻 Visit the Raintree Bookshop at **www.raintreepublishers.co.uk** to browse our catalogue and order online.

First published in Great Britain by Raintree, Halley Court, Jordan Hill, Oxford OX2 8EJ, part of Harcourt Education.
Raintree is a registered trademark of Harcourt Education Ltd.

Editorial: Diyan Leake and Richard Woodham
Design: Michelle Lisseter
Picture Research: Maria Joannou
Production: Jonathan Smith

Originated by Dot Gradations Ltd
Printed and bound in Hong Kong, China by South China Printing Company

ISBN 1 844 43673 X
08 07 06 05 04
10 9 8 7 6 5 4 3 2 1

British Library Cataloguing in Publication Data
Whitehouse, Patricia
Mixing. – (Investigations)
541.3'4
A full catalogue record for this book is available from the British Library.

Acknowledgements
The publishers would like to thank the following for permission to reproduce photographs: Corbis p. **23** (cocoa) (Richard T. Nowitz); Heinemann Library pp. **4–22** (Robert Lifson).

Cover photograph of two people cooking reproduced with permission of Corbis (Dex Images Inc.).

Every effort has been made to contact copyright holders of any material reproduced in this book. Any omissions will be rectified in subsequent printings if notice is given to the publishers.

The paper used to print this book comes from sustainable resources.

 CAUTION: Children should be supervised by an adult when handling food and kitchen utensils.

Contents

Some words are shown in bold, **like this.**
You can find them in the glossary on page 23.

What is mixing?

Mixing puts two or more things together.

When you mix some things, you can still see the parts.

When you mix some other things, you cannot see the parts.

Some things change into something new when you mix them.

Can rocks and sand mix?

Put some sand in a can.

Then add some rocks.

Put a lid on the can and shake it.

The sand and rocks are a **mixture**.

Can the mixture be separated?

Sand and rocks are mixed in the can.

You can still see both parts.

Pour the **mixture** through a screen.

You can **separate** the mixture.

Can cold water and cocoa mix?

Put some cold water in a mug.

Then add some **cocoa powder**.

Stir the water and cocoa powder.

The cocoa powder does not mix well in the cold water.

Can hot water and cocoa mix?

Ask an adult to put some hot water in a mug.

Add some **cocoa powder**.

Stir the water and cocoa powder.

The cocoa powder mixes with the hot water.

Can two different colours mix?

Put some yellow paint on a piece of paper.

Then mix in some blue paint.

The yellow and blue paint do not stay the same.

They change to make green.

Can other colours mix?

Put some red paint on a piece of paper.

Then mix in some blue paint.

Mixing red and blue paint makes purple.

Mixing two different colours makes a new one.

Can vinegar and baking soda mix?

Put some **vinegar** in a bowl.

Add some food colouring to see the vinegar better.

Then add some **baking soda**.

What happens when they mix?

Did the mixture stay the same?

The **vinegar** and **baking soda** do not stay the same.

They make bubbles.

Mixing these things causes
a **reaction**.

It makes something new –
the bubbles!

Quiz

Which two things are mixed in the can?

Look for the answer on page 24.

Glossary

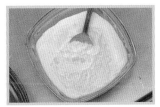
baking soda
powder used in cooking

cocoa powder
chocolate-flavour mix

mixture
when two or more things are
put together

reaction
when two or more things mix
to make something new

separate
take things apart

vinegar
sour liquid used in cooking

Index

Answer to quiz on page 22

Rocks and sand are in this mixture.

Titles in the Investigations series include:

Hardback   1 844 43670 5

Hardback   1 844 43671 3

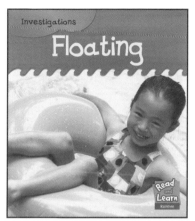

Hardback   1 844 21550 4

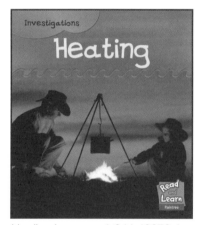

Hardback   1 844 43672 1

Hardback   1 844 43673 X

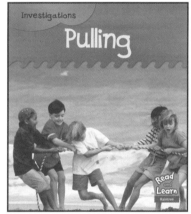

Hardback   1 844 21551 2

Hardback   1 844 21552 0

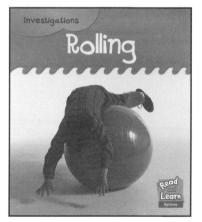

Hardback   1 844 21553 9

Hardback   1 844 21554 7

Find out about the other titles in this series on our website www.raintreepublishers.co.uk